Memory Jewelry

To: Mary Eileen

For when you have
time for memory making.

Happy Mother's Day 2010

Cathy Jakicic

Hip Handmade
Memory Jewelry

Cathy Jakicic

KALMBACH BOOKS

If you do find a few spare Euros, why not turn
birthday gift. **Choose beads that remind you of your trip.**
good substitute for Mother Nature. Some pieces benefi
of a much-loved home are a great way to wear your sentiments on your sleeve. She
her weekend lake cottage with you is a friend indeed

Kalmbach Books
21027 Crossroads Circle
Waukesha, Wisconsin 53186
www.Kalmbach.com/books

Published in 2009
13 12 11 10 09   1 2 3 4 5

Manufactured in the United States of America

ISBN: 978-0-87116-274-8

Publisher's Cataloging-In-Publication Data

Jakicic, Cathy.

   Hip handmade memory jewelry / Cathy Jakicic.

      p. : ill. ; cm.

   ISBN: 978-0-87116-274-8

1. Jewelry making—Handbooks, manuals, etc.
2. Beadwork—Handbooks, manuals, etc.
I. Title. II. Title: Memory jewelry

TT860 .J26 2009

745.594/2

Contents

them into jewelry? Charm bracelets are an easily personalized umbling small pieces of a wine or champagne bottle is a pretty greatly from miniaturization. Bangles decorated with images still keeps his letters, treasured in a safe place. A pal who shares Smooshed pennies just beg to be worn.

Introduction

dedication

To Meghan, Erin, Caty, Katy, Jenna, and Kenzie for starring in all my best memories.

The idea for this book came to me when I tagged along with a friend to scrapbooking night at her kids' grade school. I brought a bead-stringing project to work on. By the end of the night, most of the scrappers had stopped by to check it out, fascinated by the beading.

It occurred to me that, in many ways, the two passions are a lot alike. Beaders and scrappers love working with color and combining beautiful—and sometimes unexpected—elements. In both crafts, the little details are what make a project special. I realized that the memories scrapbookers mark in their scrapbook pages could be celebrated in beautiful jewelry, too.

The little details are what make a project special.

When someone sees the pieces you create with these ideas, the first thing they see will be stylish, fashionable jewelry. The memory aspect might be something only the wearer is aware of, something that makes it special to them. It's a beautiful story to tell when someone says, "Wow. What a gorgeous necklace!"

I had a great time putting this book together, partly because I got to share the experience with a lot of supportive people. I'd like to thank the friends and family that loaned me photos, mementos, and other inspiration for these projects. I'd especially like to thank my father, George Jakicic, for being an excellent editor and proofreader. Finally, I'd like to thank editor Mary Wohlgemuth and art director Lisa Bergman for their wonderful work.

I hope you enjoy the projects in *Hip Handmade Memory Jewelry* and use them to create your own modern heirlooms. Consider getting together with friends for a beading night. Sharing your creativity and stories is a great way to make a whole new set of memories.

Cathy

How to use this book

The following section includes explanations of the supplies, tools, and jewelry-making techniques that you'll need to create the projects. The techniques have been tested and refined in *BeadStyle* magazine for years, so even the newest beader can use them to get started. If a project calls for one of these basic techniques, I note it so you can refer back to pages 12–13 for review.

If a project calls for basic beads and findings, I leave it up to you to choose the specifics from your favorite store or stash. (Some projects call for supplies that are a little harder to find, and those are listed in the resource guide at the back of the book.)

The projects are grouped into four chapters: milestones, hobbies, vacations, and remembrances. Each project includes step-by-step instructions with photos. They're designed to spark your own ideas; customize them in any way you like to hold your own memories. I created my bangle bracelet project to commemorate a former home. You might use it to mark a daughter's college years.

Customize them in any way you like to hold your own memories.

As you look through the projects, you'll notice that my jewelry has a fun, slightly offbeat look. I like asymmetrical designs, for example. If that's not your thing, these projects are simple enough that a few adjustments will bring the focal point front and center.

Your memories, your jewelry. Let's get started!

Basics: materials, tools, and techniques

The materials I used for these projects encompass a broad range of beading choices—*choices* being the key word. Because most of these projects are designed around something very personal and very specific, your choice of materials may be different than mine—and that's fine.

If you're familiar with beading, you know what a wealth of options you have. For those just starting, I'm including a visual glossary of the types of beads, findings, and tools I use. Visit your local bead store, craft store, or online retailer to learn more about what's available before you begin your own projects.

I enjoy using gemstones; fire-polished, pressed, lampworked, and other glass beads; freshwater and glass pearls; and a variety of charms and pendants. You'll notice I have a particular fondness for bicone crystals. They are my go-to bead for accents, spacers, and pretty much everything else because of the broad range of colors, finishes, and sizes. I think they add class, color, and sparkle to any project.

If your tastes run to more earthy or metallic components, you can easily substitute tiny glass beads, gemstones, or metal spacers wherever I use crystals. After all, memory jewelry is all about making the pieces your own.

beads and findings

crystal and glass

bicone crystal

drop

pressed glass

round crystal

Czech fire-polished crystal

gemstone shapes

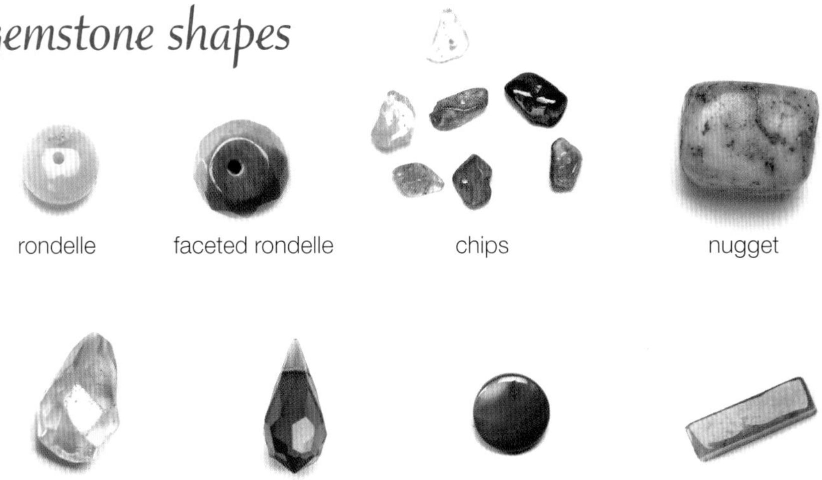

rondelle

faceted rondelle

chips

nugget

teardrop

briolette

lentil

rectangle

pearls

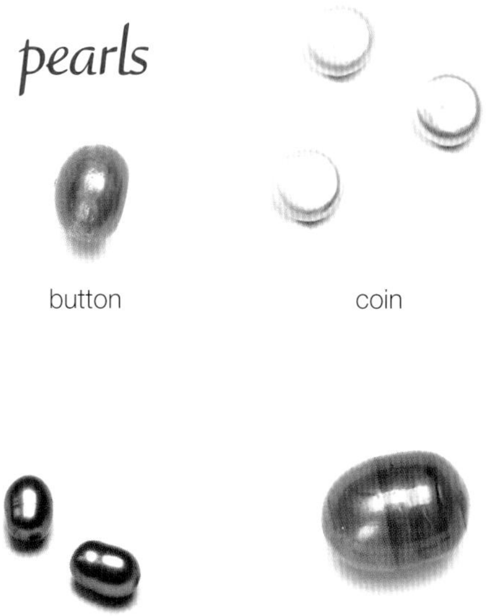

button

coin

rice

potato

findings

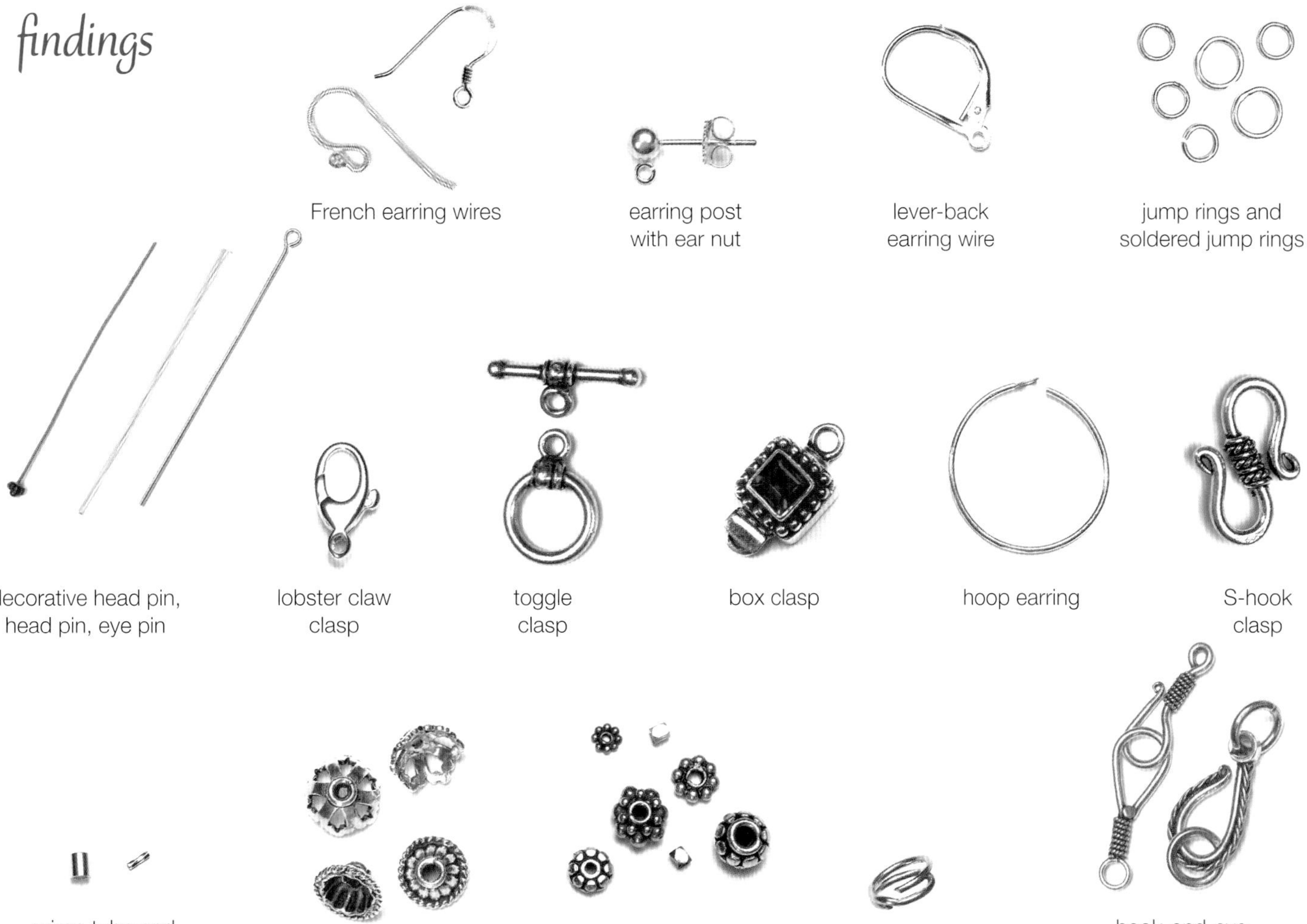

French earring wires

earring post
with ear nut

lever-back
earring wire

jump rings and
soldered jump rings

decorative head pin,
head pin, eye pin

lobster claw
clasp

toggle
clasp

box clasp

hoop earring

S-hook
clasp

crimp tube and
twist crimp

bead caps

spacers

split ring

hook-and-eye
clasps

stringing supplies

Flexible beading wire

For most stringing projects, flexible beading wire is the way to go. Flexible beading wire is made of nylon-coated strands of twisted steel. Use .010 or .012 diameter for lightweight or small-hole beads, .014 or .015 for general use, and .018, .019, or .024 for heavy beads and gemstone nuggets. (Most of the projects in this book call for .012, .014, or .015 diameter beading wire, and either 19- or 49-strand wire will work just fine.) You'll have choices of color and finish, too, so you can match the wire to your beads, wire, or other components if you choose.

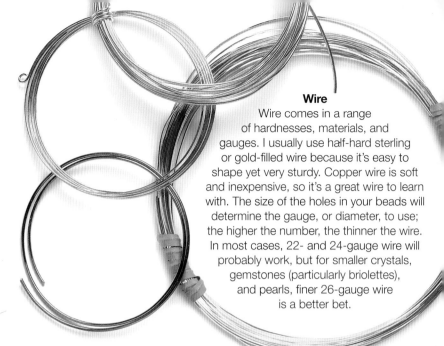

Wire

Wire comes in a range of hardnesses, materials, and gauges. I usually use half-hard sterling or gold-filled wire because it's easy to shape yet very sturdy. Copper wire is soft and inexpensive, so it's a great wire to learn with. The size of the holes in your beads will determine the gauge, or diameter, to use; the higher the number, the thinner the wire. In most cases, 22- and 24-gauge wire will probably work, but for smaller crystals, gemstones (particularly briolettes), and pearls, finer 26-gauge wire is a better bet.

Chain

The variety of chain styles grows every year, with larger-link and fancy chains becoming increasingly available. Materials range from gold-filled and sterling silver to a number of funky and fun, inexpensive base metals with finishes like copper, antique brass, and gunmetal.

additional supplies

Laminating and shrink plastic options

To turn paper images into charms and pendants, you have several choices: clear contact paper, self-laminating sleeves, or laminating film. They are pretty interchangeable. Similarly, shrink plastic is available under a number of brand names (Shrinky Dinks being the most common) and comes in clear and opaque varieties. Experiment with the materials that are easiest for you to find, and see if you have any aesthetic preferences.

Glues/sealants

Decoupage glue is great for sealing paper or wood components. It's available under a number of brand names in matte or glossy finish. I use an inexpensive, disposable foam brush to apply adhesives because I never seem to be able to completely clean a regular paintbrush of all the glue. For my shrink plastic images, I apply a matte aerosol sealant to avoid smearing the ink.

Adhesives

When a project calls for adhesive, choose a formula designed to work with a range of typical beading materials (wood, metal, and glass), such as E6000 or GS-Hypo Cement. Two-part epoxy is also a good choice.

tools

Diagonal wire cutters
are great for trimming wire, especially in very tight places. Also use them on precious metals and soft craft wires.

Roundnose pliers
have smooth, cone-shaped jaws. Use them to create loops and circles with wire or head pins.

Crimping pliers
secure the ends of projects that are strung on flexible beading wire (see folded crimp, p. 13).

For the projects in this book, use standard-size crimping pliers, which work with 2 x 2 mm and 2 x 1 mm crimp tubes.

Chainnose pliers
have long, smooth, tapered jaws for gripping, bending, squeezing, and manipulating wire and opening and closing jump rings. They're handy for flattening crimp tubes on beading wire, too (see flattened crimp, p. 13).

Split-ring pliers
A small hook on the jaws of these pliers opens a split ring so a loop or dangle can be attached.

Many of the projects use materials and tools that go beyond those typically called for in stringing projects, but all are easy to find at craft or scrapbooking suppliers.

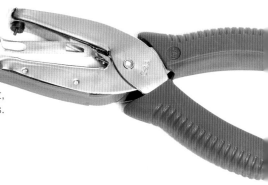

A really sharp pair of **scissors** that works with both paper and fabric is an investment you'll never regret. If you cut a lot of fabric, a second, dedicated pair is a good idea.

Eyelet setting kit
Whenever you punch a hole in a laminated component, an eyelet is a nice (though not necessary) finishing touch. Eyelets come in a number of sizes, shapes, and colors, and the setting tools are relatively inexpensive and easy to use.

A small-diameter or micro **hole punch** makes sharp, uniform holes for paper charms and pendants. Look for hole punches at scrapbooking, craft, or office supply stores.

Photos, scanners, and printers
Since all of my photos are digital, they're ready to size and print from my computer. My color laser printer makes great-quality prints, and that's what I used for most of the projects.

If you need to print onto shrink plastic, as in the Beautiful Spirits project (p. 40), use an ink-jet printer. Laser printers get too hot for the plastic film.

If you need help scanning or getting color laser prints, a shop that offers digital services (such as Kinko's) can get you started.

With the turn of a handle, a **two-hole punch** makes soft, thin metals (like coins) or plastics into jewelry components. One side creates 1.5 mm holes, which work with 16-gauge and finer wire. The other makes 2 mm holes (good for wire up to 14 gauge or other thick stringing materials).

jewelry-making techniques
plain loop

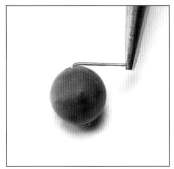

1 Trim the wire or head pin ⅜ in. (1 cm) above the top bead. Make a right angle bend close to the bead.

2 Grab the wire's tip with round-nose pliers. The tip of the wire should be flush with the pliers. Roll the wire to form a half circle. Release the wire.

3 Reposition the pliers in the loop and continue rolling.

4 The finished loop should form a centered circle above the bead.

wrapped loop

1 Make sure you have at least 1¼ in. (3.2 cm) of wire above the bead. With the tip of your chainnose pliers, grasp the wire directly above the bead. Bend the wire (above the pliers) into a right angle.

2 Using roundnose pliers, position the jaws in the bend as shown.

3 Bring the wire over the top jaw of the roundnose pliers.

4 Reposition the pliers' lower jaw snugly into the loop. Curve the wire downward around the bottom of the roundnose pliers. This is the first half of a wrapped loop.

opening and closing loops or jump rings

5 Position the chainnose pliers' jaws across the loop.

6 Wrap the wire around the wire stem, covering the stem between the loop and the top bead. Trim the excess wire and press the cut end close to the wraps with chainnose pliers.

1 Hold the loop or jump ring with two pairs of chainnose pliers or chainnose and round-nose pliers, as shown.

2 To open the loop or jump ring, bring one pair of pliers toward you and push the other pair away. Reverse the motion to close the open loop or jump ring.

making wraps above a top-drilled bead

1 Center a top-drilled bead on a 3-in. (7.6 cm) piece of wire. Bend each wire upward to form a squared-off U shape.

2 Cross the wires into an X above the bead.

3 Using chainnose pliers, make a small bend in each wire so the ends form a right angle.

4 Wrap the horizontal wire around the vertical wire as in a wrapped loop. Trim the excess wrapping wire.

folded crimp

1 Position the crimp bead in the notch closest to the crimping pliers' handle.

2 Separate the wires and firmly squeeze the crimp.

3 Move the crimp into the notch at the pliers' tip and hold the crimp as shown. Squeeze the crimp bead, folding it in half at the indentation.

4 Test that the folded crimp is secure.

flattened crimp

1 Hold the crimp using the tip of the chainnose pliers. Squeeze the pliers firmly to flatten the crimp.

2 Tug the wire to make sure the crimp has a solid grip. If the wire slides, repeat the steps with a new crimp.

split ring

To open a split ring, slide the hooked tip of split-ring pliers between the two overlapping wires.

cutting flexible beading wire

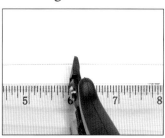

Decide how long you want your necklace to be. Add 6 in. (15 cm) and cut a piece of beading wire to that length. (For a bracelet, add 5 in./ 13 cm.)

Projects

Home fires

Very few people live in the same house their entire lives. As we move on, we leave roomfuls of memories. Bangles decorated with images of a much-loved home are a great way to wear your sentiments on your sleeve.

The blue bangle celebrates the dining room walls of my previous home, painstakingly painted (with the help of my parents) in a dark blue faux-suede pattern. I took a bunch of close-up photos of the wall before I moved and turned them into a gorgeous bracelet that can travel with me no matter how often I move.

Supplies

house bangle
- semi-dome wood bangle with eight segments
- **2–8** images sized to fit bracelet segments, approximately 1 x 2 in. (2.5 x 5 cm)
- decoupage glue
- small foam brush
- scissors

wall bangle
- wide dome wood bangle
- **1–2** pages of stamp-sized images or two full-page images
- decoupage glue
- small foam brush
- scissors

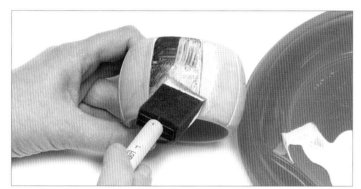

house bangle 1 Choose eight images (it's best if they are related in color). Four images used twice—or two images repeated four times—make an attractive pattern. Size and print the images, making extra copies for backup, and trim them to fit the bangle segments. Apply decoupage glue to one segment and adhere the first image. Apply a layer of glue over the entire image. Repeat for all eight segments.

2 After the glue dries, apply two more layers of glue to the entire bangle, paying particular attention to the crevices. Let the glue dry completely between coats. After the second coat dries apply a layer of glue to the inside of the bangle.

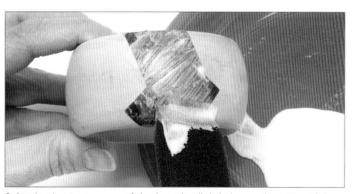

wall bangle 1 Cut out two pages of stamp-sized images or cut large images into stamp-sized segments.

2 Apply glue to an area of the bangle slightly larger than one of the images. Adhere an image and apply more glue over the image. Continue adding images in this way, layering them at different angles. Cover the bracelet completely (including the inside) and let the glue dry. Apply two more layers of glue to the entire bangle. Let the glue dry completely between coats.

Soak paper in water for a few minutes before applying to help it adhere well, especially to a curved surface. The water softens and breaks down the fibers.

One-of-a-kind charms

bracelet
and earrings

Charm bracelets are an easily personalized gift. Start with a few purchased charms and beads, and then add a few one-of-a-kind charms that truly represent the wearer.

It wasn't hard to find charms to mark things like my niece's piano playing and artistic side. To make the bracelet more personal, I created photo charms with images of Meghan, her dog, and the word *Zock*—her name for the neighborhood club she started with the purpose of making the world a better place.

bracelet 1 On a head pin, string a spacer bead, a 10 mm bead, and a spacer. Make the first half of a wrapped loop (Basics). Repeat with each bead and charm with holes.

2 Make a pencil rubbing of the bezel charm. Trim out the center oval to create a template.

3 Using the template, trace an oval around an image. Cut out the image and place it in a bezel charm.

4 Fill the bezel with glaze so the powder is slightly mounded.

5 Liquefy the glaze in an oven (or use a heat gun) according to the manufacturer's directions. Repeat steps 3–5 for all bezel charms.

Scrapbooking doodads make great charms—just glue a photo anchor to the back of an embellishment to create a loop. Considering the range of cool embellishments available from your local scrapbook supply store or online sites, your charm options are virtually endless.

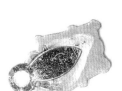

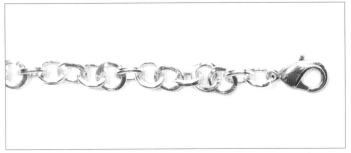

6 Cut a piece of chain to the recipient's wrist measurement plus about 1 in. (2.5 cm). Open a jump ring (Basics) and attach the lobster claw clasp to one end.

7 Plan the arrangement of the beads and charms along the chain. Leave about 1 in. (2.5 cm) empty chain on the non-clasp end.

8 Attach bead and charms with jump rings or by completing the wrapped loops.

I used two different glazing media to make the bracelet charms and the matching earrings to suggest options for you. Try both to see which you prefer.

Amazing Glaze is a great choice when you want a thick layer—it's good for deep bezels. It can be liquefied in an oven at 275°F (135°C), and it dries in a few minutes. Layering is not an option because it melts every time it's heated.

Diamond Glaze is easy to use, leaves a smooth, clear coating over nearly any material, and allows you to add many layers. Thin layers usually dry quickly, but a 1 mm layer may take several hours to dry completely, especially in high humidity.

earrings 1 As in bracelet step 3, use a template to size an image to fit the picture-frame charm. Position the image, fill the frame with glaze, and let it set according to the manufacturer's directions.

2 Open the loop of an earring wire and attach the charm. Make a second earring using a different, coordinating charm.

Sparkling birthstones

ring and
earrings

Celebrate Mother's Day or Mom's birthday with a ring that marks her birth
month along with those of her children. Crystals come in colors to represent
every birthstone. My mom was born in February (amethyst); one of her
kids was born in September (Montana to represent sapphire), and two have
December birthdays (tanzanite and turquoise), so you'll see all of those
colors in this ring I made for her. Don't be discouraged if the traditional
birthstones don't go well together. You can find options (modern, mystical,
etc.) to make it easy to create harmonious color combinations.

The matching earrings are quick and easy to make, too. They're perfect,
swingy companions for the colorful ring.

Supplies

ring
- 8 mm bicone crystal representing mom's birthday
- **21–28** 3 or 4 mm bicones representing the children's birthdays
- adjustable nine-loop ring base
- **22–29** 1-in. (2.5 cm) head pins
- chainnose pliers
- roundnose pliers
- diagonal wire cutters
- 24 in. 26-gauge wire, half-hard (optional)

earrings
- 6 3 or 4 mm bicones representing each child
- 5 in. (13 cm) chain, 3–4 mm links
- 1-in. (2.5 cm) head pin for each bicone
- 6 4 mm jump rings
- pair of earring wires
- chainnose pliers
- roundnose pliers
- diagonal wire cutters

This project translates nicely for grandmothers, too. Or say "thank you" to a great teacher by surrounding her birthstone with those of her students.

ring 1 String each crystal on a head pin. Make a plain loop (Basics).

2 Open the loop on the 8 mm bicone unit (Basics). Attach it to the center loop in the middle row of the ring base. Close the bicone unit loop.

3 Divide the remaining bicone units evenly among the remaining loops and attach. If the numbers don't allow for a perfectly even distribution, just be sure to mix up the colors and sizes of the extra bicone units as you place them around the center bicone. I show three bicone units attached to each loop. A fourth unit will fit, but it's a tight fit (and it's easier to do on outside loops).

If you want your bicone units to move easily, skip the next step—you're done!

4 Cut a 24-in. (61 cm) piece of wire. Twist one end tightly around the base of one of the ring-base loops. Holding the ring upside down so the bicone units hang straight, bind the units tightly by wrapping the wire around them several times. Turn the ring over and continue binding, adjusting the position of the units with your fingers every few wraps. Wrap the end of the wire around the base of one of the bicone units.

earrings 1 Cut the chain to these lengths: 1 in. (2.5 cm), ¾ in. (1.9 cm), and ½ in. (1.3 cm). Make bicone crystal units as in ring step 1.

2 Open a jump ring (Basics) and attach a bicone unit representing each child to the longest chain. Repeat with the other chains.

I've found ring bases

with one, three, four, five, eight, nine, and ten loops. Decide how many birthdays you want to represent, do the math, and choose a base that works for your project.

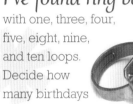

3 Open the loop on an earring wire and attach the dangles. Close the loop. Make a second earring to match the first.

The Basics section shows one method for making plain loops. Here's an alternative technique that I learned recently. For me, it's easier. Try both to see which works better for you.

1 Make a right-angle bend close to the bead. Don't trim the wire.

2 Grasp the wire with roundnose pliers near the bend and roll toward you, forming a half-circle.

3 Use your fingers to pull the tail of the wire around the lower jaw, completing the circle.

4 Cut the wire at the point just before it crosses over itself.

5 The finished loop.

Memory book

necklace and earrings

Kindergarten is a time of endless discoveries. My young friend Mackenzie was lucky enough to have a teacher who took a lot of pictures of her first classroom days. By shrinking the photos and adding them to a tiny album, school memories can be transformed into a beautiful necklace. It's perfect for Mom or as a year-end thank-you gift for that great teacher.

Even a small album makes a pretty good-sized pendant, so I recommend a longish necklace to keep things in scale—you don't want to look like you're wearing a scrapbook around your neck. This necklace looks great layered with other long chains or necklaces.

necklace 1 Choose the photos for your album. I needed an image for the cover and one for every lower page in the album. (I kept the upper pages open for journaling by the recipient.) Size the images. For a 2½-in. (6.4 cm) square page, I made 1¾-in. (4.4 cm) square images. Print extra "just in case" copies.

2 Open the album cover. Trace the outline onto the wrong side of the contact paper. Add a narrow margin (about ¼ in./6 mm) for folding. Trim the paper and remove the backing. Center the album on the sticky side of the contact paper and carefully fold over the excess. Make short, angled cuts in the contact paper on the fold lines as shown.

My album cover has flaps and a cutout window. I opened the flaps and covered the whole thing with contact paper. I cut an X in the contact paper for the window.

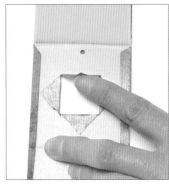

3 Fold the contact paper flaps to the inside around the window.

4 With a micro hole punch, punch a hole at the top and bottom of every page (including the cover). The cover of my album already had holes, but the inside pages did not. I used the cover holes as a guide for the rest of the holes.

5 On the inside of the cover, apply glue around the window. Position an image behind the window and adhere.

6 Apply glue to the back of an image and center it on a book page. Repeat for all the pages.

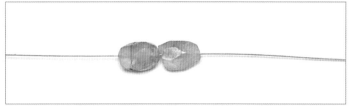

7 Cut a piece of beading wire (Basics). Center two oval beads on the wire.

8 On each end, string a pattern of four briolettes, an oval, and four briolettes. Repeat twice.

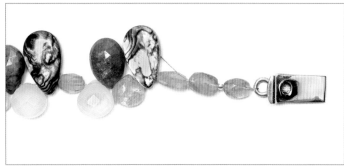

9 On each end, string ovals until the strand is within 1 in. (2.5 cm) of the desired length. On each end, string a crimp bead, an oval and half of a clasp. Go back through the beads just strung. Check the fit and add or remove beads if necessary. Tighten the wires and flatten or crimp the crimp beads (Basics). Trim the excess wire.

10 Cut a 4-in. (10 cm) piece of 24-gauge wire. Center a briolette and make a set of wraps above the bead (Basics). Make a wrapped loop (Basics).

11 Open a 10 mm earring hoop and attach the dangle.

The mini album I used had a ribbon accent, which I removed before applying the contact paper. If you'd like, you can make your own album by using heavy card stock for the cover and lightweight paper for the inside. Cut the cover and pages to the finished width and twice the finished height (the album is oriented vertically as a pendant). Fold the pages in half and staple along the fold.

12 Using three different briolettes, make three dangles, following step 10. Attach them to a second hoop.

13 Use the three-dangle hoop to attach the book to the beaded strand. Use the other earring hoop as a closure for the book.

Using earring hoops instead of jump rings makes it easier to open and close the book and to remove and reattach the book to the beaded strand.

earrings Make matching earrings by following step 10 of the necklace instructions and attaching the dangles to 20 mm earring hoops.

Gifts of style

necklace and earrings

Almost every woman I know made rolled magazine-paper beads at some point in her youth. The beads in this set are the grown-up version. They're the perfect keepsake made from wedding or wedding shower gift wrap, which is usually thick, in elegant colors and patterns. It makes great beads.

For the necklace, I elongated the triangles to get a round bead instead of the rice-shaped beads of my youthful endeavors. Heavy paper helps with this, too. You can string an entire necklace with these beads, but I find they're effective as accents for similarly sized coin pearls. I used the classic rice shape for the earrings.

Supplies

necklace 16 in. (41 cm)
- wrapping paper, 3 x 20 in. (7.6 x 51 cm)
- 16-in. (41 cm) strand 12 mm coin pearls
- **32–36** 3 mm bicone crystals
- flexible beading wire, .012
- **2** crimp beads
- toggle clasp
- chainnose pliers
- roundnose pliers
- diagonal wire cutters
- 1–2 mm diameter rod
- decoupage glue
- small foam brush
- crimping pliers (optional)
- small paintbrush (optional)
- acrylic paint (optional)

earrings
- wrapping paper, 2 x 16 in. (5 x 41 cm)
- **2** 12 mm coin pearls
- **4** 3 mm bicone crystals
- 4 in. 22-gauge wire, half-hard
- **2** 2-in. (5 cm) head pins
- pair of earring wires
- chainnose pliers
- roundnose pliers
- diagonal wire cutters

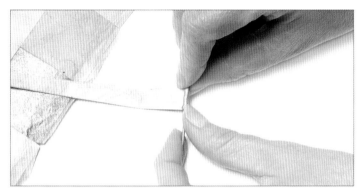

necklace 1 Cut a 20-in. (51-cm) triangle that is ½ in. (1.3 cm) wide at its base. Starting at the base, tightly roll the paper around the rod, keeping the narrow end centered as you roll. Occasionally apply a dab of glue as you roll. Apply glue to the entire last 4 in. (10 cm). Apply a layer of glue to the whole bead to seal it before you remove it from the rod. Make a total of six beads.

2 Cut a piece of beading wire (Basics, p. 12). On the wire, center a coin pearl and a 3 mm bicone crystal.

3 On each end, string an alternating pattern of three bicones and three paper beads.

4 On each end, string an alternating pattern of bicones and pearls until the strand is within 1 in. (2.5 cm) of the finished length. String an equal amount of pearls and bicones on each end to center the wrapping paper beads. If you'd prefer them off center (as I do) string about a third more beads on one side.

On each side, string a crimp bead, a bicone, and half of a clasp. Check the fit and add or remove beads if necessary. Go back through the beads just strung. Tighten the wires and flatten or crimp the crimp beads (Basics). Trim the excess wire.

If your bead doesn't have as much color as you'd like, you can cheat by adding dabs of paint before sealing with the final coat of glue.

It's the nature of the rolled paper bead that no two will be exactly alike, especially if you use textured paper. Don't drive yourself nuts trying to make them exactly alike. Embrace their uniqueness.

earrings 1 Following step 1 of the necklace instructions, roll a paper bead from a 16-in. (41 cm) triangle that is 1 in. (2.5 cm) wide at its base. Cut a 2-in. (5 cm) piece of wire. Make a plain loop at one end, string the bead, and make a plain loop above the bead.

2 On a head pin, string a 3 mm bicone crystal, a pearl, and a bicone. Make the first half of a wrapped loop (Basics).

3 Attach the pearl unit to a plain loop on the paper bead unit and finish wrapping the loop. Open the loop of an earring wire, attach the dangle, and close the loop. Make a second earring to match the first.

Rewards bracelet

Does your favorite fourth grader have 30 books to read this semester? Do you have 20 pounds to lose before the class reunion? These success bracelets are stylish motivation for anyone with a long-term goal. Short-term, they mark progress with a bead reward for every small positive step. In the long run, they become a beautiful, lifelong reminder of a goal accomplished. The key is removable end pieces that allow the gradual addition of beads.

bracelet 1 Decide on the number of steps toward the goal and the number of beads to mark each step. Cut one loop of memory wire. String a bead and attach a Scrimp to one end of the memory wire.

2 If you don't want beads to slide around before the goal is reached, center them on the wire between two Scrimps. For each step toward the goal, remove one Scrimp and add a bead or beads. Reattach the Scrimp. Consider stringing a larger bead every fifth step to mark a mini milestone.

3 When the goal is reached, trim any extra memory wire. You can add a thematic charm as a final celebration of success.

Supplies

- 4 mm bicone crystals (enough to mark the steps toward the goal)
- bracelet-size memory wire
- **2–4** Scrimp beads
- Scrimp screwdriver or tiny eyeglass screwdriver
- heavy-duty wire cutters or chainnose pliers
- 6–8 mm rondelles (enough to mark small milestones along the way—optional)
- charm representing the goal (optional)

The Scrimp bead stoppers have tiny screws that can be tightened (or loosened) around beading wire.

No heavy-duty wire cutter? Trim memory wire by bending it back and forth repeatedly with chainnose pliers. Never use regular wire cutters on memory wire.

The memory wire version is a good fit for small wrists. For adults, attractive cuffs like this one, which has removable ends, are available.

Sea glass celebration

I love the look of sea glass, but tumbling small pieces of a wine or champagne bottle is a pretty good substitute for Mother Nature. What better way to commemorate a champagne occasion than to transform the bottle into an elegant necklace? An inexpensive, child-friendly rock tumbler smoothed the pieces into perfect "sea glass," and an easy-to-use drill turned the pieces into beads.

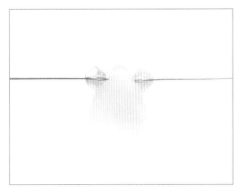

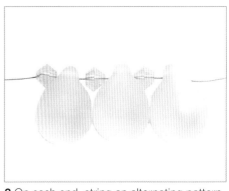

necklace 1 Cut a piece of beading wire (Basics). Center a bicone crystal, a teardrop bead, and a bicone.

2 On each end, string an alternating pattern of sea-glass beads and bicones.

3 On each end, string an alternating pattern of teardrops and bicones until the strand is within 1 in. (2.5 cm) of the finished length.

4 On each end, string a crimp bead, two bicones and half of a clasp. Check the fit and add or remove beads if necessary. Tighten the wires and flatten or crimp the crimp beads (Basics). Trim the excess wire.

Tumbling and drilling was easy, thanks to some equipment designed for kids (see Resources, p. 93). I put the bottle in a thick plastic bag, sealed it, and hit it with a hammer until the pieces were the sizes I liked (it's smart to wear safety glasses while you're doing this). Then I tumbled the glass, letting the tumbler run for four days.

A safe, affordable child's rock drill worked perfectly to create holes in my "sea glass." If you prefer a shortcut (although you won't have the pleasant memory of emptying the bottle!), buy imitation sea glass—you can find it already drilled into beads.

Supplies

necklace 16 in. (41 cm)
- **12** sea-glass beads
- **2** 4-in. (10 cm) strands
  14 mm teardrop beads
- **52** 4 mm bicone crystals
- flexible beading wire, .012
- **2** crimp beads
- toggle clasp
- chainnose or crimping pliers
- diagonal wire cutters

earrings
- **8** 14 mm teardrop beads
- **2** 4 mm bicone crystals
- **8** in. (20 cm) 24-gauge wire,
  half-hard
- pair of earring wires
- chainnose pliers
- roundnose pliers
- diagonal wire cutters

If you don't want to drill holes in the bottle glass, a simple set of wire wraps will work, too. Cut a piece of 20-gauge wire long enough to wrap around the "sea glass" twice with 3 in. (7.6 cm) left over.

1 Start with one end of the wire at the top of the glass and wrap the wire around twice vertically. Tuck the wire end under the second wrap.

2 Make a wrapped loop (Basics) at the top and continue wrapping around the glass, further securing the vertical wraps.

Earring alternative

earrings 1 Cut a 4-in. (10 cm) piece of 24-gauge wire. String a teardrop bead and make a set of wraps above the bead (Basics).

2 On the wire, string a bicone and three teardrops. Make a wrapped loop above the beads and trim the excess wire.

3 Open the loop of an earring wire, attach the dangle, and close the loop. Make a second earring to match the first.

Great performances

necklace and
earrings

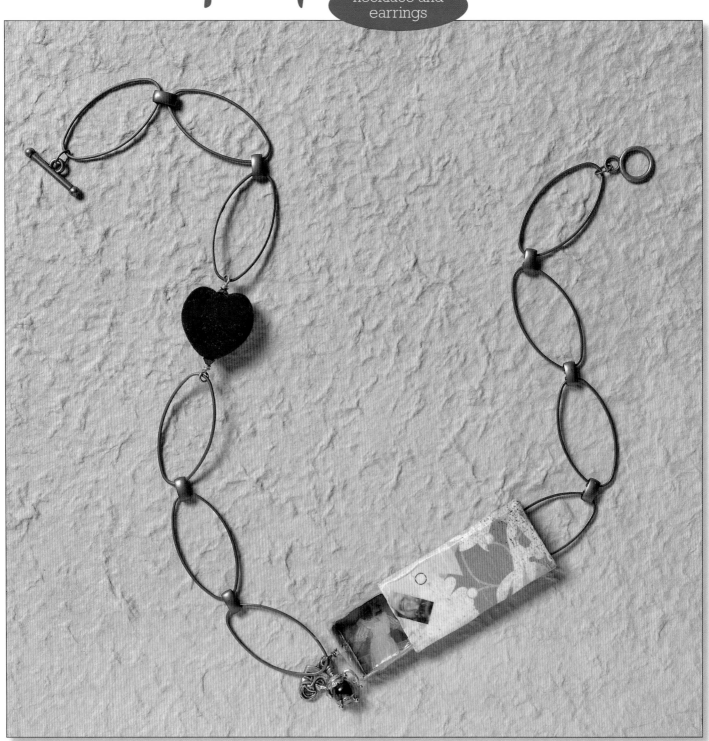

I love to see the pride of accomplishment on the faces of special young "stars" when I attend their plays or recitals. This necklace commemorates my friend Katy's lead role in her eighth-grade production of *Alice in Wonderland*. The pendant holds an image from the play, visible when the matchbook "curtain" is open. I added a tiny picture of the leading lady to the outside of the pendant, and chose accent beads to reflect the play's theme.

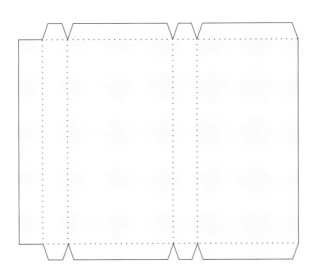

necklace 1 This template fits a matchbox that is 1⅛ x 2⅛ x ¼ in. (2.9 x 5.4 cm x 3 mm). Adjust the template to fit your matchbox, if necessary, and draw or trace onto the wrong side of the patterned card stock. Trim on the solid lines. Score and fold on the dotted lines.

Supplies

necklace 22 in. (56 cm)
- matchbox with drawer
- image from performance sized to fit inside of matchbox
- ¼–½ in. (6 mm–13 cm) black-and-white photo of "star"
- 2.5 cm accent bead
- **1** sheet patterned heavy card stock to match accent bead
- 17–19 in. (43–48 cm) chain, 1½-in. (3.8 cm) links
- 4 in. (10 cm) 22-gauge wire, half-hard
- **2** 6 mm jump rings
- **2** 2-in. (5 cm) head pins
- toggle clasp
- chainnose pliers
- roundnose pliers
- diagonal wire cutters
- decoupage glue
- acrylic paint
- small foam brush
- small paintbrush
- scissors
- micro hole punch (optional)
- **2** charms with jump rings or head pins (optional)

earrings
- **2** 1-in. (2.5 cm) accent beads
- **4** 4 mm bicone crystals
- **2** 1½ -in. (3.8 cm) links
- **2** 2-in. (5 cm) head pins
- pair of earring wires
- chainnose pliers
- roundnose pliers
- diagonal wire cutters

2 Apply a thin layer of decoupage glue to one outside panel of the matchbox. Position the trimmed card stock and adhere. Continue adhering all the panels in this way. Finish by tucking and gluing the narrow end flaps to the inside of the box.

3 Apply two more layers of decoupage glue to the outside of the cover, letting the glue dry thoroughly between applications.

4 Apply two thin layers of acrylic paint to the drawer of the matchbox. Let the paint dry between coats.

5 Print and trim two images: one to fit the inside bottom of the matchbox and a close-up black-and-white photo of the star.

6 Apply a thin layer of glue to the inside bottom of the drawer and position the large image.

7 Adhere the close-up photo to the outside of the matchbox cover.

8 Poke a head pin through one end of the drawer from the inside (the micro hole punch helps here). Make the first half of a wrapped loop (Basics). Repeat on the other end of the drawer.

9 Cut a 4-in. (10 cm) piece of wire and make the first half of a wrapped loop. String a bicone, an accent bead, and a bicone. Make the first half of a wrapped loop (Basics).

10 Cut two 5-in. (13 cm) pieces of chain. Attach one chain to each loop on the accent bead unit and complete the wraps.

38

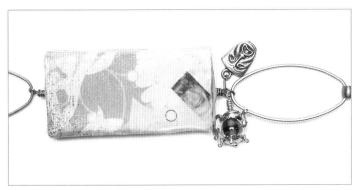

11 Attach the open loop on one end of the drawer to the strand from step 10. Complete the wraps. Cut a 7-in. (18 cm) piece of chain and attach to the remaining open loop on the drawer. Complete the wraps. Attach charms to one of the loops if desired.

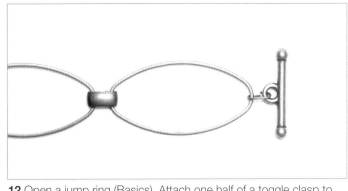

12 Open a jump ring (Basics). Attach one half of a toggle clasp to one end. Close the jump ring. Repeat on the other end.

earrings 1 On a head pin, string a bicone crystal and an accent bead. Make a plain loop (Basics).

2 Cut one link of chain. Open the plain loop (Basics) of the bead unit, attach it to the link, and close the loop. Open the loop on an earring wire. Attach the dangle and close the loop. Make a second earring to match the first.

If you prefer a shorter earring, skip the big chain link and attach the dangle directly to an earring wire.

Beautiful spirits

necklace and
earrings

I like to think we pick role models primarily for their inner beauty. But no matter how we choose, portraits of our heroes and heroines can become beautiful jewelry. Make a necklace as a gift to inspire a new graduate, or anyone (including yourself) who could use a reminder of a guiding spirit.

necklace 1 Using an ink-jet printer, print the image on the rough side of a sheet of shrink plastic. Punch a hole in the top and shrink according to package directions. A 3-in. (7.6 cm) image shrinks to about 1¼ in. (3.2 cm) square. Spray with sealant. Let dry.

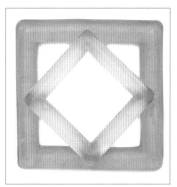

2 Glue the two frames together as shown. Let dry.

3 Cut a 3-in. (7.6 cm) piece of wire. String the shrink plastic image and the frame on the wire. Make a set of wraps above the frame (Basics). Make a wrapped loop perpendicular to the frame.

4 Cut a piece of beading wire (Basics). Center the pendant on the wire.

When the plastic shrinks, it may not stay flat. You can flatten it by hand when it's still warm, but you risk smudging the ink; by the time the ink is dry and smudge-free, the plastic is no longer malleable. For the perfectionist, this creates a dilemma: not-quite-flat or slightly smudged. I chose the first option because the frames better camouflage that flaw.

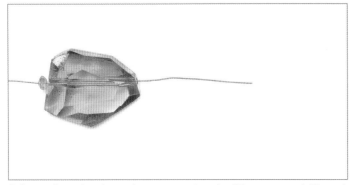

5 On each end, string a 4 mm nugget and a 25 mm nugget. Repeat until the strand is within 1 in. (2.5 cm) of the finished length.

6 On each end, string a 5 mm round spacer, a crimp bead, a spacer, and half of a clasp. Check the fit and add or remove beads if necessary. Go back through the beads just strung, tighten the wires, and flatten or crimp the crimp beads (Basics). Trim the excess wire.

I used glass frames and nuggets, but other materials— gemstones, metal, plastic, wood—work just as well in this design.

earrings 1 Following necklace steps 2 and 3 (minus the shrink-plastic image), make a dangle, keeping the loop parallel to the frames.

2 Open the loop of an earring wire. Attach the dangle and close the loop. Make a second earring to match the first.

Backpack tag

These speedy tags are a perfect way to personalize a school backpack, a young dancer's gear bag, or a proud mom's tote. Just a slide a photo into a luggage tag blank and add some fun beads. Personalize it further by adding a quote or comment to the photo.

Supplies

- 2½ x 4 in. (6.4 x 10 cm) image
- **2–6** novelty or accent beads (make sure at least 2 are larger than the tag opening)
- **2** 2-in. (5 cm) head pins
- 2 in. cable chain, 2–3 mm links
- luggage tag blank
- chainnose pliers
- roundnose pliers
- diagonal wire cutters
- scissors

I used my word-processing program to add text to my image. Rub-on letters are also a good option. If you're confident in your lettering skills, just use a fine-point felt-tip pen on the image.

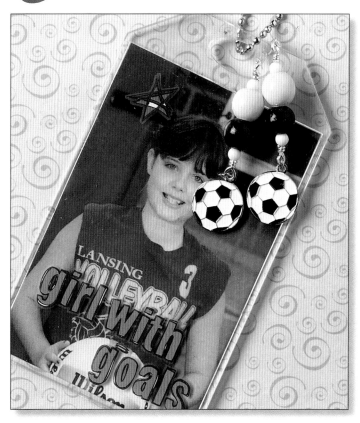

1 Trim the finished image to fit the luggage tag.

2 Insert the image into the tag and snap the cover closed. If desired, add identifying info such as names and dates to the back before closing the cover.

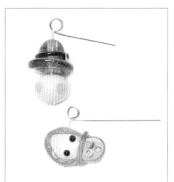

3 On a head pin, string 1–3 novelty beads. Make the first half of a wrapped loop (Basics). Repeat with second head pin.

4 String a 2-in. (5 cm) piece of chain through the opening of the tag. Attach a dangle to each end of the chain and complete the wraps.

Pop culture necklace and earrings

I'm always amazed how bits of popular culture, such as a certain movie or song, can carry so much meaning and trigger so many memories. It's easy to turn these memories into great jewelry because movie posters and album or CD covers are often works of art in themselves. Let your image inspire your choice of beads.

necklace 1 Cut out your pendant image. Use a micro hole punch to punch a hole in the top of the image.

2 Cut a piece of laminating film slightly larger than the image. Remove the backing from the film and center the image face down on the sticky side. Smooth the image to remove wrinkles or air pockets.

3 Punch the hole again.

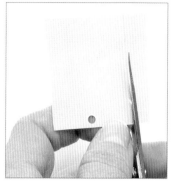

4 Trim the film to the size of the image. Back the image with another piece of laminating film and punch the hole again.

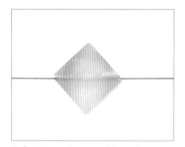

5 Cut two pieces of beading wire (Basics). Cut the second piece 1 in. (2.5 cm) longer than the first. On the shorter wire, center a diamond-shaped bead.

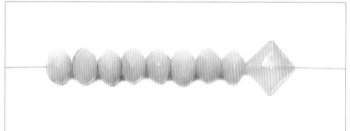

6 On each end, string eight rondelles and a diamond.

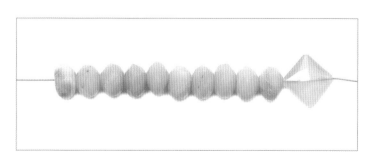

7a On each end, string 10 rondelles and a diamond

7b Repeat steps 6 and 7a, omitting the last diamond. Set the strand aside.

I repunched the hole in the pendant at each stage because going through only one layer results in a cleaner punch hole.

Supplies

**necklace 17–18 in.
(43–46 cm)**

- small image (1¼ x 1¾ in./
  3.2 x 4.4 cm)
- sheet of laminating film
- 16-in. (41 cm) strand,
  20 mm oval beads
- 16-in. (41 cm) strand,
  12 mm diamond-shaped
  beads
- 16-in. (41 cm) strand
  8 mm rondelles
- flexible beading wire, .014
  or .015
- 6 mm jump ring
- **4** twist crimp beads
- box clasp
- chainnose pliers
- roundnose pliers
- diagonal wire cutters
- micro hole punch
- scissors

earrings

- **2** 20 mm oval beads
- **2** 12 mm diamond-shaped
  beads
- **2** 8 mm rondelles
- 2¼ in. (5.7 cm) cable chain,
  3 mm links
- **4** 1½-in. (3.8 cm) head pins
- pair of earring wires
- chainnose pliers
- roundnose pliers
- diagonal wire cutters

8 Open a jump ring (Basics).
Attach the pendant and close
the jump ring. Center the
pendant on the longer wire.

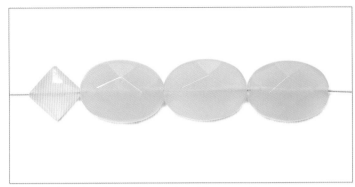

9 On each end, string a diamond and three oval beads.
Repeat twice.

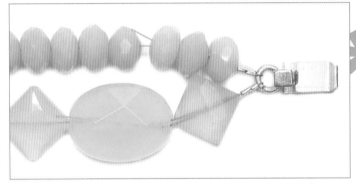

10 On each end of the longer wire, string a diamond, an oval, a
diamond, a twist crimp bead, and half of a clasp. On each end of
the shorter strand, string a twist crimp and half of the clasp. Check
the fit and add or remove beads if necessary. Tighten the wires and
flatten the crimp beads (Basics). Trim the excess wire.

*The twist-style
crimps* in this
necklace (Twisted
Tornado is the
brand name) add
an elegant finishing
touch, and they're
very secure. Simply
flatten the tube with
chainnose pliers.

Put a bit of tape (or use Bead Stoppers) on the ends
of the first strand while you work on the second.

earrings 1 On a head pin, string an oval bead and make a wrapped loop (Basics). On another head pin, string a diamond-shaped bead and a rondelle. Make the first half of a wrapped loop.

2 Cut a 1-in. (2.5 cm) piece of chain. Attach the chain to the diamond-rondelle unit and complete the wraps.

3 Open the loop of an earring wire (Basics). Attach the dangle and the oval bead unit. Close the loop. Make a second earring to match the first.

Cool fridge art

necklace and earrings

While the refrigerator door is a time-honored venue for the display of youthful artistic endeavors, unless you mount exhibitions in your kitchen, it offers limited exposure. Turning fridge art into a resin pendant is quick, easy, and a great way to showcase your budding Monet. And frankly, some pieces benefit greatly from miniaturization.

necklace 1 Trim your image to fit and place in the mold. Mix the resin according to the kit instructions. Use a toothpick to position the image, if necessary, and let the resin harden.

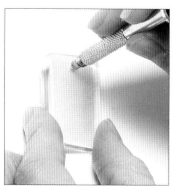

2 Remove the hardened resin component from the mold. Use the mini drill from the kit to pierce a hole near the top.

3 On a head pin, string a 4 mm bicone crystal and the pendant. Bend the head pin at a right angle where it exits the resin component. Make a wrapped loop (Basics) perpendicular to the pendant.

4 Cut a piece of beading wire (Basics). Center the pendant on the wire.

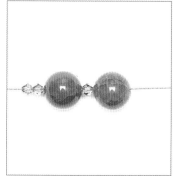

5 On each end, string two bicones, a 12 mm round bead, a bicone, and a round. Repeat the pattern until the strand is within 1 in. (2.5 cm) of the finished length, ending with two bicones.

6 On each end, string a crimp bead, a bicone, and half of a clasp. Check the fit and add or remove beads if necessary. Go back through the beads just strung. Tighten the wires and crimp the crimp beads (Basics). Trim the excess wire.

earrings 1 On a head pin, string a 4 mm bicone crystal, a 12 mm round bead, and a bicone. Make a wrapped loop (Basics).

2 On an earring hoop, string two bicones, the dangle, and five bicones. Use chainnose pliers to bend back the tip of the hoop. Make a second earring to match the first.

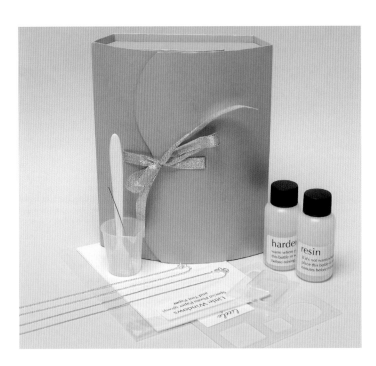

The resin kit I used was the Little Windows Photo Make-3 Jewelry Kit. I bought a rectangular mold on the Little Windows Web site (square molds were included with the kit). If you plan to make a lot of pendants, purchase larger quantities of resin; one option is the Colores brand from Rio Grande.

Although I used the mini drill included with the kit, you can use a rotary tool or power drill with a tiny bit to make a small hole in the hardened resin.

Garden variety

necklace and earrings

The glories of a well-tended garden are beautiful but fleeting. Capture a bit of the foliage forever for a friend with a green thumb or to commemorate your own collaboration with nature.

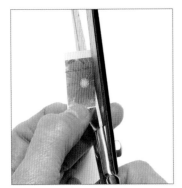

necklace 1 Trim an image to fit a frame.

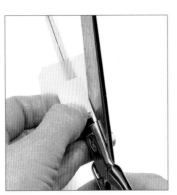

2 Cut a piece of laminating film slightly larger than the image. Remove the backing from the film. Center the image face down on the sticky side of the film. Smooth the image to remove wrinkles or air pockets. Trim the laminating film to the size of the image.

3a Slide the laminated image into a frame. Apply a dot of glue to secure the image to the frame if needed.

3b Open a jump ring (Basics), attach a frame charm, and close the jump ring. Repeat for each charm.

4 Cut a piece of beading wire (Basics). On the wire, string a frame charm and a 3 mm spacer.

5 On one side, string an 8 mm pearl, a spacer, and a flower charm.

6 On the other side, string: 8 mm pearl, spacer, flower charm, 8 mm, spacer, frame charm, 8 mm, spacer, flower, 8 mm, spacer, frame, 8 mm, spacer, flower.

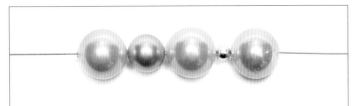

7 On each side, string: 8 mm pearl, 6 mm pearl, 8 mm, spacer, 8 mm. Repeat the pattern until the strand is within 2 in. (5 cm) of the finished length.

8 On each end, string two 6 mm pearls, a crimp bead, a 6 mm, and half of a clasp. Check the fit and add or remove beads if necessary. Tighten the wires and flatten or crimp the crimp beads (Basics). Trim the excess wire.

earrings 1 Cut a 2½-in. (6.4 cm) piece of 24-gauge wire. Make a wrapped loop (Basics). String an 8 mm pearl and make another wrapped loop.

Supplies

necklace 16 in. (41 cm)
- **3** frame charms
- **3** garden images to fit frames
- sheet of laminating film
- **4** flower charms
- 16-in. (41 cm) strand 8 mm glass pearls
- 16-in. (41 cm) strand 6 mm glass pearls
- **19–23** 3 mm round spacers
- flexible beading wire, .014 or .015
- **7** 6 mm jump rings
- **2** crimp beads
- box clasp
- chainnose pliers
- roundnose pliers
- diagonal wire cutters
- crimping pliers (optional)
- adhesive (optional)

earrings
- **2** frame charms
- **2** garden images to fit frames
- sheet of laminating film
- **2** flower charms
- **2** 8 mm glass pearls
- 5 in. (13 cm) 24-gauge wire, half-hard
- **2** 6 mm jump rings
- pair of earring wires
- chainnose pliers
- roundnose pliers
- diagonal wire cutters
- adhesive (optional)

2 Create framed images as in necklace steps 1–3a. Open a jump ring (Basics). Attach the pearl unit, a flower charm, and a frame charm. Close the jump ring.

3 Open the loop of an earring wire. Attach the dangle and close the loop. Make a second earring to match the first.

Best sellers

bracelet and earrings

My book club just celebrated its 20th anniversary. In that time, we have read nearly 150 great books (and a few clunkers). To celebrate the anniversary, I gathered the covers of some of my favorite titles in this bracelet.

bracelet 1 Cut a book image for every large link in the chain. Position images on a self-laminating sheet and seal according to package directions. Cut out each image leaving ⅛ in. (3 mm) of plastic around the edges.

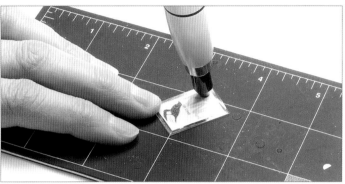

2 Using a micro hole punch, make a hole in an upper corner of each image. If desired, secure an eyelet in each hole according to the setting kit instructions.

3 On a head pin, string a pearl and a silver bead. Make the first half of a wrapped loop (Basics). Make a silver bead unit for each large link in the chain.

4 Open a jump ring (Basics) and attach a book charm and a large link. Close the jump ring.

5a Attach a silver bead unit to the same large link. Complete the wraps.
5b Repeat steps 4 and 5a for every large link.

6 On each end, open a split ring and attach an end link and half of a clasp.

Making these bracelets and earrings is a great activity for a book club meeting—even for those who aren't beaders. Have each member bring her own images; you supply the rest of the materials and your beading expertise.

Supplies

bracelet
- **10–12** book cover images, sized to approximately ½ x 1 in. (1.3 x 2.5 cm)
- self-laminating sheet
- **10–12** 10 mm silver accent beads in two shapes
- **10–12** 4 mm freshwater pearls
- 6–7 in. (15–18 cm) large-and-small link chain
- **10–12** 6 mm jump rings
- **10–12** 1½-in. (3.8 cm) head pins
- **2** 8 mm split rings
- box clasp
- chainnose pliers
- roundnose pliers
- split ring pliers (optional)
- diagonal wire cutters
- micro hole punch
- **10–12** eyelets (optional)
- eyelet setting kit (optional)

earrings
- **2** book cover images, sized to approximately ½ x 1 in. (1.3 x 2.5 cm)
- self-laminating sheet
- **2** 10 mm silver accent beads
- **4** 4 mm freshwater pearls
- 6 in. (15 cm) 24-gauge wire, half-hard
- pair of earring wires
- chainnose pliers
- roundnose pliers
- diagonal wire cutters
- micro hole punch
- **2** eyelets (optional)
- eyelet setting kit (optional)

earrings 1 Following bracelet steps 1 and 2, make a book charm. Cut a 3-in. (7.6 cm) piece of wire. Make a wrapped loop (Basics). String a pearl, a silver bead, and a pearl. Make the first half of a wrapped loop.

2 Attach the book charm and the half-wrapped loop. Complete the wraps. Open the loop of an earring wire and attach the dangle. Make a second earring to match the first.

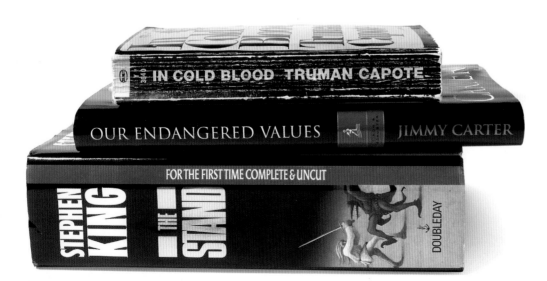

vacations

Euro chic

necklace and earrings

I find it amazing that anyone returns from a European vacation with any money at all. But if you do find a few spare Euro coins, why not turn them into jewelry? It's lot more interesting than tossing them into a jar to await your next journey. Use small, light coins to minimize the weight.

This necklace recalls my effort to exchange larger coins for centimes using my less-than-adequate French. Painful for all involved, I'm sure, but the resulting jewelry made it worthwhile, *n'est-ce pas*?

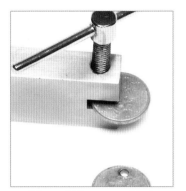

necklace 1 Use a metal hole punch to pierce the top of each coin.

2 On a head pin, string a 4 mm color A bicone, a 14 mm octagonal bead, and 4 mm A bicone. Make the first half of a wrapped loop (Basics).

3 On a head pin, string: 3 mm A bicone, 3 mm C bicone, 12 mm faceted barrel bead, 4 mm B bicone. Make the first half of a wrapped loop. Make a total of six barrel units.

4 On a head pin, string a 4 mm C bicone, a 10 mm oval glass bead, and a 4 mm C bicone. Make the first half of a wrapped loop. Make a total of 12 oval units.

5a Cut a 24-in. (61 cm) piece of 6 mm-link cable chain.

5b Open a jump ring (Basics) and attach a coin to the center link on the chain. Close the jump ring. If your coins aren't all the same size, string the larger ones in the center of the strand.

6a On each side, attach an alternating pattern of three oval units and three coins as shown. Complete the wraps and close the jump rings as you go.

6b Cut a 20-in. (51 cm) piece of 6 mm-link chain. Following steps 5b and 6a, attach coins and oval units.

7 Cut a 22-in. (56 cm) piece of 4 mm-link cable chain. Open a jump ring (Basics) and attach the octagonal unit to the center link on the chain. Complete the wraps. On each side, attach an alternating pattern of three coins and three barrel units as shown. Complete the wraps and close the jump rings as you go.

Supplies

**necklace 20–24 in.
(51–61 cm)**
- **20–25** coins
- **14** mm octagonal bead
- **6** 12 mm faceted barrel beads
- **12** 10 mm oval glass beads
- **2** 4 mm bicone crystals, color A
- **24** 4 mm bicone crystals, color B
- **6** 4 mm bicone crystals, color C
- **6** 3 mm bicone crystals, color A
- **6** 3 mm bicone crystals, color C
- **44** in. (1.1 m) cable chain, 6 mm links
- **22** in. (56 cm) cable chain, 4 mm links
- **20–25** 6 mm jump rings
- **19** 2-in. (5 cm) head pins
- toggle clasp
- chainnose pliers
- roundnose pliers
- diagonal wire cutters
- metal hole punch

earrings
- **2** coins
- **2** 10 mm oval glass beads
- **4** 4 mm bicone crystals, color B
- **22** in. (15 cm) 22-gauge wire, half-hard
- **8** 6 mm jump rings
- lever-back earring wires
- chainnose pliers
- roundnose pliers
- diagonal wire cutters
- metal hole punch

Coin collectors

generally discourage people from cleaning their coins as it can diminish their value, but I'm guessing they have no plans to wear them. Check out **coins. thefuntimesguide.com** (search on "cleaning") for a nice selection of cleaning techniques. To keep the coins shiny after your hard work, apply a protective coating like an archival wax or spray sealant.

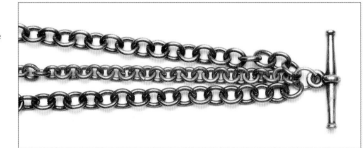

8 Open a jump ring and attach one end of each strand to half of a toggle clasp, arranging them from shortest to longest. Close the jump ring. Repeat on the ends of the remaining strands with the other clasp half.

earrings 1 Following necklace step 1, punch a hole in a coin. Cut a 3-in. (7.6 cm) piece of wire. Make a wrapped loop (Basics). String a 4 mm color B bicone, a 10 mm oval bead, and a 4 mm B bicone. Make a wrapped loop.

2 Open a jump ring (Basics). Attach a coin to the oval-bead unit. Close the jump ring.

3 Open the loop on an earring wire (Basics). Attach the dangle and close the loop. Make a second earring to match the first.

Notebook charm

SUPER-QUICK PROJECT

Before summer ends, use some of your best vacation snapshots to make some of these popular notebook charms with or for your young friends. The swivel clips link these bookmarks to spiral notebooks, day planners, or anything else with a wire or ring spine.

Supplies

- small image
- enough 4 mm beads or crystals for a 3–4-in. (7.6–10 cm) strand
- 12–15 mm accent bead
- flexible beading wire, .014 or .015
- 7 mm split ring
- **2** crimp beads
- swivel clip
- sheet of laminating film
- chainnose or crimping pliers
- diagonal wire cutters
- scissors
- micro hole punch
- split ring pliers (optional)

For a two-sided photo charm, use decoupage glue to adhere two photos back-to-back before laminating.

1 Follow laminating directions from the "Pop culture" project (p. 44). Attach a split ring (Basics).

2 Cut an 8-in. (20 cm) piece of beading wire. On the wire, center an accent bead. On each end, string 4 mm beads until the strand is the desired length.

3 On one end, string a crimp bead and the photo charm. Repeat on the other end, substituting the swivel clip for the charm. Go back through the beads just strung. Tighten the wires and flatten or crimp the crimp beads (Basics). Trim the excess wire.

Weekend to remember

necklace and
earrings

A pal who shares her weekend lake cottage with you is a friend indeed. Send this thank-you message in a bottle—a tiny container of sand with key charm. If you're lucky enough to have your own beach house, this necklace makes a great welcome-to-the-lake present for a new neighbor.

necklace 1 Fill bottle ¾ full with sand. Insert key charm. Apply glue to the cork and close the bottle. For an optional bit of color, wrap a piece of colored craft wire around the bottle, twist the ends together, and trim the excess wire.

2 Cut a 7½-in. (18 cm) piece of chain. Open a jump ring (Basics) and attach the bottle charm to the center of the chain. Close the jump ring.

3 Cut two 11-in. (28 cm) pieces of flexible beading wire. On each wire, string 7 in. (18 cm) of an alternating pattern of oval beads and rondelles.

4 On one end of each strand, string a twist crimp, a rondelle, and one end of the chain. Go back through the beads just strung and flatten the crimp (Basics). Trim the excess wire.

5 On the other end of each strand, string a twist crimp, a rondelle, and half of a clasp. Check the fit and add or remove beads if necessary. Go back through the beads just strung and flatten the crimp. Trim the excess wire.

Did you know it's illegal in many places to take sand from a public beach? You should probably stick to sand from private property or pick up a small bag of playground sand.

Supplies

necklace 23 in. (58 cm)
- 25 mm glass bottle charm
- 2 tsp. sand
- tiny key charm
- 16-in. strand (41 cm) 13 mm oval beads
- 16-in. strand (41 cm) 8 mm rondelles
- 7½ in. (19.1 cm) cable chain, 20 mm links (reserve 2 links for earrings)
- flexible beading wire, .014 or .015
- 7 mm jump ring
- **4** twist crimp beads
- toggle clasp
- chainnose pliers
- roundnose pliers
- diagonal wire cutters
- E6000 adhesive
- 2 in. (5 cm) colored craft wire (optional)

earrings
- **2** 13 mm oval beads
- **2** 20 mm links from cable chain
- **2** 1½-in. (3.8 cm) head pins
- **2** 7 mm jump rings
- pair of earring wires
- chainnose pliers
- roundnose pliers
- diagonal wire cutters

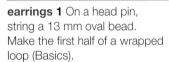

earrings 1 On a head pin, string a 13 mm oval bead. Make the first half of a wrapped loop (Basics).

2 Attach the bead unit to a 20 mm link and complete the wraps.

3 Open a jump ring (Basics). Attach the dangle and the loop of an earring wire. Close the jump ring. Make a second earring to match the first.

I skipped the sand bottles for the earrings because they get a bit heavy.

Cent-imental style

My second-favorite vacation souvenir is the smooshed penny. My favorite always has been plastic injection-molded figurines, but those are kind of big for jewelry. Smooshed pennies, however, just beg to be worn. Add copper accents and an eclectic collection of beads for a beautiful necklace-and-earring set. I used pennies from many trips, but if you plan ahead and keep your eyes peeled for the smooshing machines, you can collect enough pennies to have your jewelry represent a single great vacation.

necklace 1 Use a metal hole punch to pierce the narrow ends of each penny.

2 On head pins, string beads and bead caps in five different configurations as shown. Make the first half of a wrapped loop (Basics) on each bead unit. Make a total of 15 bead units.

3 Cut three 3-in. (7.6 cm) pieces and three 4-in. (10 cm) pieces of chain. Open two jump rings (Basics) and attach a 3-in. and a 4-in. chain to a smooshed penny. Close the jump rings. Continue attaching pennies and chains, alternating the 3-in. and 4-in. chains.

4 On each 4-in. chain, attach three different dangles, spacing them evenly between the pennies. Complete the wraps.

5 Attach one each of the remaining dangles on a 3-in. chain in the same way. Repeat with the remaining dangles and chains.

6 On each end, attach half of a clasp with a jump ring.

For a funkier look, mix different finishes of chain and findings instead of using all copper.

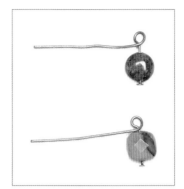

earrings 1 String a lentil bead on a head pin and make the first half of a wrapped loop (Basics). Repeat with a flat square bead.

Supplies

necklace 29½ in. (74.9 cm)
- **5** smooshed pennies
- **3** 14 mm oval copper beads
- **3** 10 mm round beads
- **3** 8 mm flat square beads
- **3** 8 mm flat round beads
- **3** 8 mm round Czech glass beads
- **3** 6 mm round beads
- 22 in. (56 cm) copper cable chain, 6 mm links
- **12** 6 mm copper bead caps
- **12** 6 mm copper jump rings
- **15** 1½-in. (3.8 cm) copper head pins
- copper toggle clasp
- chainnose pliers
- roundnose pliers
- diagonal wire cutters
- metal hole punch

earrings
- **2** smooshed pennies
- **2** 8 mm flat square beads
- **2** 8 mm lentil beads
- **7** links of copper cable chain, 6 mm links
- **2** 6 mm copper jump rings
- **4** 1½-in. (3.8 cm) copper head pins
- pair of earring wires
- chainnose pliers
- roundnose pliers
- diagonal wire cutters
- metal hole punch

2 Cut a three-link piece of chain, attach the lentil bead unit, and complete the wraps.

3 Following necklace step 1, punch holes in a smooshed penny. Attach a flat square bead unit and complete the wraps.

4 Attach both dangles to the earring wire. Pinch the wire closed. Make a second earring to match the first.

Penny smooshing, smashing, squishing, pressing, elongating—whatever you call it, this activity has legions of online fans. Before your next trip, check out **pennycollector.com** (click on **locations**) to find pressing machine sites across the U.S. and all over the world.

Vacation fan

Venetian beads and a few images of the countryside are beautiful reminders of a picturesque trip to Italy. Acrylic tags from the scrapbook store serve as segments of the fan. I forced myself to choose only three images, but it's possible to string more using a bigger jump ring. The resulting necklace will get pretty heavy, though, so a little discipline will pay off. If your necklace doesn't have an Italian accent, skip the Venetian beads and use beads you bought during your trip or that complement the colors in your photos.

Supplies

necklace 16½–20 in. (41.9–51 cm)
- **3** acrylic tags (1 x 2 in./ 2.5 x 5 cm)
- **3** vacation images trimmed to fit tags
- **2** 13 mm Venetian disk beads
- **2** 6 mm Venetian cube beads
- **3** 4 mm spacer beads
- 9 in. (23 cm) 22-gauge wire, half-hard
- 34 in. (86 cm) long-and-short chain, 22 mm and 7 mm links
- 15 mm jump ring
- **4** 6 mm jump rings
- **4** 2-in. (5 cm) head pins
- two-loop box clasp
- chainnose pliers
- roundnose pliers
- diagonal wire cutters
- decoupage glue
- small foam brush
- gold metallic paint (optional)
- small paintbrush (optional)

earrings
- **2** 6 mm Venetian cube beads
- **2** 2-in. (5 cm) head pins
- 5 in. (13 cm) long-and-short chain, 22 mm and 7 mm links
- pair of earring wires
- chainnose pliers
- roundnose pliers
- diagonal wire cutters

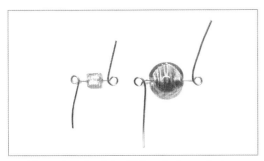

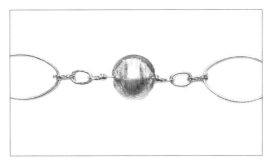

necklace 1 Cut a 3-in. (7.6 cm) piece of wire. Make the first half of a wrapped loop (Basics). String a Venetian disk bead and make the first half of a wrapped loop. Repeat with the remaining Venetian beads.

2 Cut two 7½-in. (19.1 cm) pieces of chain. Attach each chain to the half loop of a disk-bead unit. Complete the wraps.

3 Cut the remaining chain into three pieces: 2 in. (5 cm), 5½ in. (14 cm), and 11½ in. (29.2 cm). Attach each end of the short chain to half loops on the remaining bead units. Complete the wraps. Attach the long chain to the remaining half loop on the cube-bead unit. Attach the remaining chain to the remaining loop on the disk bead unit. Complete the wraps.

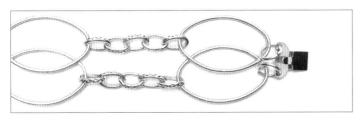

4 Open two jump rings (Basics). Using the jump rings, attach one end of each chain to a loop on half of a clasp. Repeat with the other half of the clasp.

If you'd rather center the fan pendant and make symmetrical bead-and-chain segments, you'll need an extra disk bead and an extra cube bead.

5 Use decoupage glue to adhere each trimmed image to an acrylic tag. Seal the image with another layer of glue. (Try not to get the glue on the uncovered acrylic. If you do, wait till it dries and scrape it off.) If desired, paint the edges and other exposed acrylic with gold metallic paint. (I used Liquid Leaf.)

6 Open a 15 mm jump ring. Attach the tags.

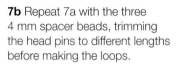

7a On a head pin, string a cube bead. Trim the head pin to 1 in. (2.5 cm) and make a plain loop at the end.

7b Repeat 7a with the three 4 mm spacer beads, trimming the head pins to different lengths before making the loops.

8 String the dangles on the 15 mm jump ring above the tags. Attach the jump ring to the longer strand opposite the disk bead. Close the jump ring.

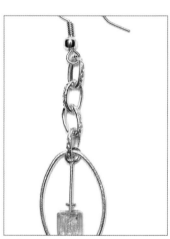

earrings 1 Cut a piece of chain consisting of four small links and one large link. Following necklace step 7a, make a cube bead dangle. Open the plain loop on the dangle and attach it to the large link and the adjacent small link. Close the loop.

2 Open the loop on an earring wire. Attach the dangle and close the loop. Make a second earring to match the first.

City girl

necklace and earrings

You just visited Paris, Madrid, San Francisco, Manhattan, or Sheboygan, and it's your new favorite city. Declare your love for all to see with a simple decoupaged map bead. String it as an off-center centerpiece in a simply stunning necklace. I used rough-cut gemstones to complement the uneven texture of the bead. Make quick matching earrings using extra gemstones or a thematically appropriate charm.

Supplies

necklace 17½ in. (44.5 cm)
- map with chosen city prominently marked (size of print must fit on bead)
- 25 mm wooden bead
- 16-in. (41 cm) strand, 12–21 mm rough-cut gemstones
- **25–29** 4 mm bicone crystals
- flexible beading wire, .014 or .015
- 2 crimp beads
- S-hook clasp
- chainnose pliers
- roundnose pliers
- diagonal wire cutters
- decoupage glue
- small foam brush
- scissors
- crimping pliers (optional)

earrings
- **2** charms
- **2** 4 mm bicone crystals
- 2 in. (5 cm) 20-gauge wire
- pair of earring wires
- chainnose pliers
- roundnose pliers
- diagonal wire cutters

necklace 1 Cut the map into pieces small enough to shape around the bead but large enough to retain some detail. Make sure one piece clearly shows the name of the city. Decoupage the pieces onto the wooden bead following the directions from the "Home fires" project (p. 16). Leave the bead holes open. Adhere the name of the city last, centering it between the holes. Let dry.

2 Cut a piece of beading wire (Basics) and string the bead.

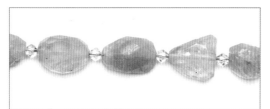

3 On each end, string an alternating pattern of gemstones and 4 mm bicone crystals until the strand is within 1 in. (2.5 cm) of the finished length. String more gemstones and crystals on one end so the decoupaged bead is off center.

4 On each end, string a crimp bead, a bicone, and half of a clasp. Check the fit and add or remove beads if necessary. Go back through the beads just strung. Tighten the wires and flatten or crimp the crimp beads (Basics). Trim the excess wire.

earrings
1 Cut a 1-in. (2.5 cm) piece of wire. Make a plain loop (Basics). String a 4 mm bicone crystal and make a plain loop.

2 Open a loop on the bicone unit (Basics), attach the charm, and close the loop. Open the loop of an earring wire, attach the dangle, and close the loop. Make a second earring to match the first.

Memory chips

necklace and
earrings

I learned about Photofetti from a friend when I was looking for something special for my parents' 50th anniversary. Photofetti is double-sided round photo confetti mixed with colorful accent pieces. The photo chips are 1 in. (2.5 cm) in diameter. Upload up to 10 photos on photofetti.com and you get 450 pieces of confetti altogether.

I've been wanting to turn this novel memento into jewelry ever since the anniversary party. This necklace-and-earring set is autobiographical, a collection of photos from my childhood—so far, my most photogenic period.

Supplies

necklace 18–19 in. (46–48 cm)

- **19–25** Photofetti chips in three sizes
- **2** 16-in. (41 cm) strands 10 mm oval glass beads in two colors
- 16-in. (41 cm) strand 6 mm nuggets
- **2** 16-in. (41 cm) strands 4 mm nuggets
- **24** 4 mm flat spacers
- flexible beading wire, .014 or .015
- **19–25** 6 mm jump rings
- **6** twist crimp beads
- three-strand box clasp
- chainnose pliers
- roundnose pliers
- diagonal wire cutters
- clear contact paper
- scissors
- micro hole punch

earrings

- **6** Photofetti chips in three sizes
- **2** 6 mm jump rings
- pair of earring wires
- chainnose pliers
- roundnose pliers
- clear contact paper
- scissors
- micro hole punch

necklace 1 Choose the Photofetti chips you want to use (including a few extra just in case). Peel the backing from a piece of contact paper large enough to accommodate all the chips and place the chips on the paper. Peeling the backing off as you go, carefully roll a second sheet of contact paper over the first so the sticky sides meet.

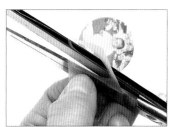

2 Cut out each chip as close to the edge as possible.

3 Using the micro hole punch, punch a hole in the top of a chip. Open a jump ring and attach the chip (Basics). Close the jump ring. Repeat for each chip.

Even the smallest pack of Photofetti has many more chips than you need for a necklace-and-earring set. Because you have up to 10 photo uploads, you can send multiple themes with two to four photos each. You could make gifts for a number of people from one Photofetti pack.

4 Cut a piece of beading wire (Basics). Cut a second piece 1 in. (2.5 cm) longer and a third piece 2 in. (5 cm) longer than the first. Center a photo chip on the mid-length wire.

5 On each end of the mid-length wire, string five 4 mm nuggets and a large accent chip.

6 On each end, string: five 4 mm nuggets, photo chip, five 4 mm nuggets, small accent chip, and enough 4 mm nuggets until the strand is within 1 in. of the finished length.

7 Center a photo chip on the short strand.

Use a fingernail, coin, or craft stick to burnish the chips for the clearest possible image behind the contact paper.

8 On each end, string a 4 mm nugget, a 10 mm oval bead, a 6 mm nugget, and a large accent chip.

9 On each end, repeat the bead pattern from step 8, string a photo chip, and repeat the bead pattern until the strand is within 1 in. (2.5 cm) of the finished length.

10 Follow steps 8–9 to string the long strand, using the second oval bead color and adding a small accent chip to the pattern.

11 On each end of each strand, string two spacers, a twist crimp, two spacers, and half of a clasp. Check the fit and add or remove beads if necessary. Tighten the wires and flatten the crimp beads (Basics). Trim the excess wire.

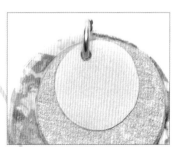
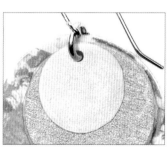

earrings 1 Following necklace steps 1–3, make a photo chip, a large accent chip, and a small accent chip. Instead of attaching a jump ring to each chip, string all three chips on one jump ring in descending order of size.

2 Open the loop on an earring wire (Basics). Attach the dangle and close the loop. Make a second earring to match the first.

The partially covered photo chip becomes just a pattern rather than a recognizable image.

Baby clothes swatch

necklace and
earrings

Baby clothes are so cute—and so temporary. Kids outgrow them or make them otherwise unwearable before you know it. But if you salvage just a scrap, you can make a pendant to remind them (or you) of their onesie period. This necklace was made from an outfit from the closet of the very stylish Miss Caroline Force Cahill. It's nice to think in a dozen years or so she may wear this reminder of her carefree youth.

Supplies

necklace 16 in. (41 cm)
- 1 x 1 in. (2.5 cm) fabric swatch
- frame charm, ¾ x ⅞ in. (1.9 x 2.2 cm)
- 16-in. strand 8 mm faceted rondelles
- **36** 5 mm nuggets
- **10** 5 mm flat spacers
- **8** 3 mm spacer nuggets
- flexible beading wire, .014 or .015
- 7 mm jump ring
- **2** crimp beads
- lobster claw clasp and 7 mm soldered jump ring
- fabric stiffener
- chainnose or crimping pliers
- diagonal wire cutters
- scissors

earrings
- **2** 8 mm faceted rondelles
- **6** 5 mm nuggets
- 2 in. (5 cm) 22-gauge wire, half-hard
- **6** 2-in. (5 cm) head pins
- pair of earring wires
- chainnose pliers
- roundnose pliers
- diagonal wire cutters

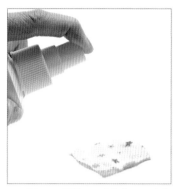

necklace 1 Trim a fabric swatch to fit a frame charm. Spray the swatch with fabric stiffener and let it dry.

2 Slide the swatch into the frame. Use a pin to guide it, if necessary.

3 Open a jump ring (Basics), attach the charm's loop, and close the jump ring. Cut a piece of beading wire (Basics). On the wire, center a 3 mm spacer nugget, the frame, and a spacer nugget.

4 On each end, string nine 5 mm nuggets.

5a On each end, string a 5 mm flat spacer, a 8 mm faceted rondelle, and a flat spacer.

5b Repeat steps 4 and 5a.

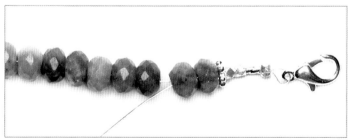

6 On each end, string rondelles until the strand is within 1 in. (2.5 cm) of the finished length. On one end, string: flat spacer, two spacer nuggets, crimp bead, spacer nugget, lobster claw clasp. Repeat on the other side, substituting a soldered jump ring for the clasp. Check the fit and add or remove beads if necessary. Go back through the beads just strung. Tighten the wires and flatten or crimp the crimp beads (Basics). Trim the excess wire.

A collection of frames with baby clothes swatches from siblings make a great charm bracelet for a mom or grandmother. For ideas on how to put it together, refer to the charm bracelet project on p. 18.

earrings 1 Cut a 1-in. (2.5 cm) piece of wire. Make a plain loop (Basics). String an 8 mm faceted rondelle. Make a plain loop.

2 On a head pin, string a 5 mm nugget. Make a plain loop at the end of the head pin. Repeat with two more head pins, trimming each ¼ in. (6 mm) shorter than the last before making the plain loop.

3 Open a plain loop on the rondelle unit and attach the three head pin units. Close the loop. Open the loop of an earring wire. Attach the dangle and close the loop. Make a second earring in the mirror image of the first.

Timeless treasure

My grandmother was a working mom before the term existed. When she retired from the box factory after 40-plus years, she was given a small watch and a modest pension. Although the watch may have been a humble farewell gift, it is a proud symbol of the kind of woman she was and a great frame for the photo pendant created in her memory.

necklace 1 Remove the band and inner working from the watch.

2 Cut the photo to fit and position it in the watch "frame." Add a drop or two of adhesive as needed to secure the back, and reattach it to the frame.

3 Cut a 3-in. (7.6 cm) piece of wire. String a 14 mm crystal briolette. Make a set of wraps above the bead (Basics). Make the first half of a wrapped loop above the wraps (Basics).

4a Cut a two-link piece of chain. Attach the chain to the briolette unit and complete the wraps.

4b Open a jump ring (Basics) and attach the dangle to the bottom of the watch pendant. Close the jump ring.

5 On a head pin, string a 4 mm bicone crystal. Make the first half of a wrapped loop. Make three bicone units.

6 On a head pin, string two bicones. Make a wrapped loop. Make six two-bicone units, leaving the loops unwrapped on two of the units.

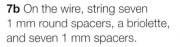

7a Cut a 9-in. (23 cm) piece of beading wire.

7b On the wire, string seven 1 mm round spacers, a briolette, and seven 1 mm spacers.

8 On each end, string a 3 mm round spacer, a two-bicone unit, and a 3 mm round spacer.

9 Repeat steps 7b, 8, and 7b again on each end. Cut two 8½-in. (21.5 cm) pieces of chain. On each end of the beaded strand, string a 3 mm spacer, a crimp bead, a 3 mm spacer, and the end link of a chain. Go back through the beads just strung. Tighten the wires and flatten or crimp the crimp beads (Basics). Trim the excess wire.

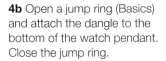

For extra significance, use a crystal color that represents the birthstone of the person featured in your pendant.

10 Cut a 25-in. (63.5 cm) piece of chain. Using a jump ring, attach one end of both chains and half of a clasp. Repeat on the other side with the other clasp half. Check the fit, and add or remove an equal number of links from each end, if necessary.

11a Using a jump ring, attach the watch unit to the center link of the longer chain.

11b Attach three bicone units to the two-link chain and complete the wraps.

11c Attach a two-bicone unit to the link on each side of the pendant. Complete the wraps.

Supplies

necklace 22½–25 in. (54.5–63.5 cm)
- watch casing
- photo sized to fit in watch
- **6** 14 mm faceted crystal briolettes
- **15** 4 mm bicone crystals
- **10** 3 mm round spacers
- **70** 1 mm round spacers
- 3 in. (7.6 cm) 24-gauge wire, half-hard
- 42 in. (107 cm) cable chain, 5 mm links
- **2** crimp beads
- **4** 10 mm jump rings
- **9** 1½-in. (3.8 cm) head pins
- toggle clasp
- chainnose pliers
- roundnose pliers
- diagonal wire cutters
- scissors
- E6000 adhesive
- crimping pliers (optional)

earrings
- **2** 14 mm faceted crystal briolettes
- **6** 4 mm bicone crystals
- 3 in. (7.6 cm) 24-gauge wire, half-hard
- 1 in. (2.5 cm) cable chain, 5 mm links
- **6** 1½-in. (3.8 cm) head pins
- pair of earring wires
- chainnose pliers
- roundnose pliers
- diagonal wire cutters

earrings 1 Following necklace steps 3, 4a, 5 and 11b, make a briolette dangle.

2 Open the loop of an earring wire. Attach the dangle and close the loop. Make a second earring to match the first.

Heartfelt words

My mom lost a beloved uncle in World War II. She still treasures his letters and keeps them in a safe place. I photocopied his parting words and encased them in a box pendant she can wear close to her heart.

You can make this pendant even if you don't have a handwritten quote. Just type meaningful words in an attractive font on cream-colored paper for an old-time feel. Subtly colored gemstones and lampworked glass beads create a vintage look in both the necklace and matching earrings.

Supplies

necklace 17½ in. (44.5 cm)
- quotation on slip of paper, 3 x ¾ in. (7.6 x 1.9 cm)
- open-box pendant (1 x ¾ in. /2.5 x 1.9 cm)
- clear plastic sheet protector
- 16-in. (41 cm) strand, 12 mm lampworked square pillow-shaped beads
- **12** 8 mm flat square beads
- **34** 6 mm disk beads, drilled off-center
- **8** size 11° seed beads
- flexible beading wire, .014 or .015
- 4–5 in. (10–13 cm) of narrow fabric ribbon
- 10 mm jump ring
- **2** crimp beads
- toggle clasp
- chainnose pliers
- roundnose pliers
- diagonal wire cutters
- scissors
- glue

earrings
- **2** open-box pendants (½ x ¼ in./1.3 x .6 cm)
- **2** 8 mm flat square beads
- **6** 6 mm disk beads, drilled off-center
- 4 in. (10 cm) 22-gauge wire, half-hard
- pair of earring wires
- chainnose pliers
- roundnose pliers
- diagonal wire cutters

necklace 1 Print and trim the quote you want to use to ¾ x 3 in. (1.9 x 7.6 cm).

2 Tightly roll the quote with the printed side facing out. Tie the paper with a fabric ribbon. Trim the ribbon close to the knot.

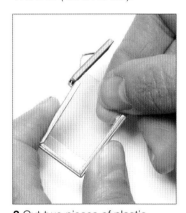

3 Cut two pieces of plastic sheet protector to fit the box pendant. Apply glue to the corners of the pendant to secure the plastic.

4 When the glue is dry, insert the quote and close the pendant.

5 Cut a piece of beading wire (Basics). Open a jump ring (Basics) and attach it to the loop of the pendant. Close the jump ring. Center the pendant on the wire.

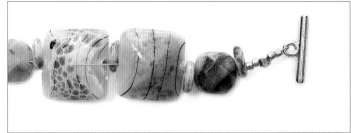

6 On each end, string: 6 mm disk bead, 12 mm lampworked bead, disk bead, 8 mm flat square bead, disk bead. Repeat the pattern until the strand is within 1 in. (2.5 cm) of the finished length.

7 On each end, string two 11° seed beads, a crimp bead, two 11°s, and half of a clasp. Check the fit and add or remove beads if necessary. Go back through the beads just strung, tighten the wires, and flatten or crimp the crimp beads (Basics). Trim the excess wire.

You can encase a sentimental word or two in the earrings as well. Follow necklace step 3 to add plastic walls to the pendants.

earrings 1 Cut a 2-in. (5 cm) piece of wire. Make a wrapped loop (Basics). String a 6 mm disk bead, an 8 mm flat square bead, and two disks. Make the first half of a wrapped loop.

2 Attach the box pendant to the open loop and complete the wraps.

3 Open the loop of an earring wire. Attach the dangle. Close the loop. Make a second earring to match the first.

Make memories your own

necklace and earrings

My nieces are fascinated by my jewelry, just as I was mesmerized by the jewelry my grown-up relatives wore when I was a child. If we're lucky enough to be given jewelry by women we admire, chances are those valued pieces will get a lot more use if they are updated a bit. I took some jewelry that had been sitting in a drawer for years and added glass pearls for a look that's all mine. A few extra beads made quick earrings.

necklace 1 Cut two pieces of beading wire (Basics). Cut one piece 1 in. (2.5 cm) longer than the other. On the longer wire, string a 2½-in. (6.4 cm) pattern of vintage beads.

2 On one end, string a 3¼-in. (8.3 cm) pattern of vintage beads. On the other end, string a 2¾-in. (7 cm) pattern of the same beads.

3 One one end, string five 10 mm glass pearls. On the other end, string glass pearls until the strand is within 1 in. (2.5 cm) of the finished length.

Vintage Lucite beads make attractive additions to your remade inherited pieces. The range of colors available is wider and brighter than glass pearls.

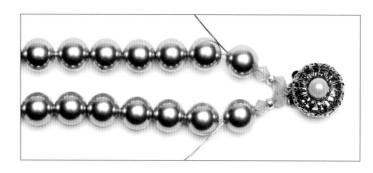

4 On the shorter strand, string a sequence of beads similar to the one strung in steps 1–3. Make the second strand 1 in. (2.5 cm) shorter than the first. Arrange the strands so the longer glass pearl segments are on different sides.

5 On each end of each strand, string a bicone, a crimp bead, a bicone, and the loop of half a clasp. Go back through the beads just strung. Check the fit and add or remove beads if necessary. Tighten the wires and crimp or flatten the crimp beads (Basics). Trim the excess wires.

The costume jewelry necklaces

I started with were strung with cultured South Sea pearls and round glass beads.

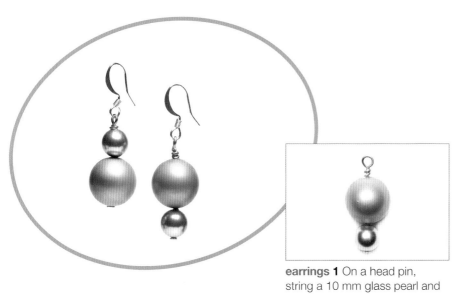

earrings 1 On a head pin, string a 10 mm glass pearl and a vintage glass bead. Make a wrapped loop (Basics).

2 Open the loop of an earring wire, attach the dangle, and close the loop. Make a second earring by stringing a glass bead and then a pearl, and finishing in the same way as the first.

Baby blankie

Giving up a baby blanket can be a traumatic event. Without naming names, I've seen baby blankets that travel on business trips with successful adults. I have no solution for the Linuses among us, but their female counterparts can turn the remains of beloved blankies into cute woven bracelets with a comforting hippie feel. The bracelet can be a comforting gift for a kid facing blanket separation anxiety, too.

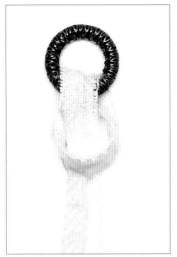

1 Spray the fabric strip with fabric stiffener to limit fraying. Fold the strip in half and tie a lark's head knot around a hoop.

2 Tie a half-hitch knot with the left-hand strip of fabric.

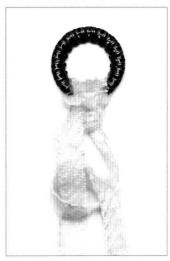

3 Tie a half-hitch with the right-hand strip of fabric.

4 String a pearl on the left-hand strip of fabric and repeat step 2.

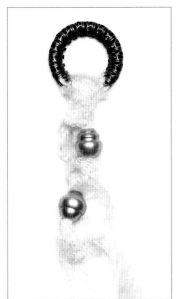

5 Repeat step 3, string a pearl on the left-hand strip of fabric and repeat step 2. Continue stringing pearls on alternate strips and repeating steps 2 and 3 until the bracelet is the desired length.

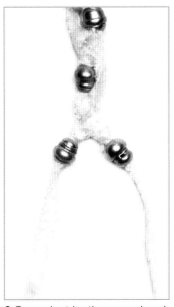

6 On each strip, tie an overhand knot, string a pearl, and tie an overhand knot.

7 String a pearl on each strip and tie an overhand knot 4 in. (10 cm) from the last knot. Trim the excess fabric.

Supplies

- 51–60-in. (1.3–15 m) strip of baby blanket fabric, ¼–½ in. (6–1.3 mm) wide
- 23 mm hoop
- **10–12** large-hole, 10 mm potato pearls
- fabric stiffener

To wear the bracelet, pull the ends through the hoop and adjust to fit your wrist.

Friendship rings

SUPER-QUICK PROJECT

A young friend of mine got a ring-making kit for a birthday gift. Following the instructions, she painted colors on the reverse of clear, flat-backed plastic gems and glued them to a ring base. I liked her results, and took the idea a step further by incorporating tiny, sentimental images. The domed gems remind me of mini snow globes. I love wearing and sharing these rings to recall good friends and good times.

1 Trim the photo so a tiny border is visible around the photo when positioned on the gem.

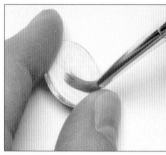
2 Apply a thin layer of decoupage glue to the back of the gem. Position the photo and apply another thin layer of glue to the back. Let dry.

3 Put a dot of adhesive on the center of the gem and attach the ring back. Let dry.

Supplies

- flat-backed glass or plastic gemstones
- image reduced to fit behind gem
- ring base with flat surface
- scissors
- decoupage glue (or any clear-drying glue)
- E6000 adhesive
- scrapbook photo anchor, jump ring, and charm (optional)

To add a charm

Before you do step 3, glue a photo anchor (see p. 19) between the gem and the ring base so only the loop is visible. Attach a charm to the loop with a jump ring.

The smaller ring base in the photo at right is from my friend's Opti-Art rings kit (**creativityforkids.com**). The inexpensive kit included 10 adjustable rings and 12 clear plastic gems. The larger ring is silver-plated brass (**store.swarovski-crystallized.com**). Flat-backed glass gems in a variety of sizes can be found at **megaglass.com**.

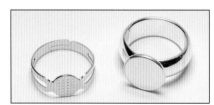

Resources

Here's a guide to finding some of the more unusual supplies I used throughout the book. See the list on the next page for the Web sites for these suppliers and others.

Home fires
wood bangles Hobby Lobby

One-of-a-kind charms
cabochon settings Ornamentea
snap-close jump rings Via Murano
flower picture-frame pendants, charm pendant Fusion Beads

Memory book
Kolo Mini Mini photo album Paper Source or kolo.com

Sea glass celebration
rock tumbler The Gem Shop
rock drill Museum Tour Catalog

Cool fridge art
resin jewelry kit Little Windows

Backpack tag
luggage tag blank, Irish beads Oriental Trading Co.

Garden variety
frame charms Eclectica, Oriental Trading Co.

Euro chic
metal hole punch Fire Mountain Gems

Notebook charm
swivel clip Fire Mountain Gems

Weekend to remember
tiny key charm Ornamentea

Cent-imental style
metal hole punch Fire Mountain Gems

Vacation fan
acrylic tags Legacy Scrapbooks
Venetian beads Bella Venetian Beads

Baby clothes swatch
frame charm Oriental Trading Co.

Heartfelt words
open-box pendant Ornamentea

Make memories your own
vintage components Chelsea's Beads

Baby blankie
hoop Vintaj Natural Brass Co.

Resources

To gather supplies for making your own memory jewelry, try your local bead, scrapbooking, or craft store. They're great places to get inspiration and ask questions, and it's important to support them. I also do some of my shopping online. The sites below are good places to start.

A. C. Moore acmoore.com

Absolute Crystal Components absolutecrystalcomponents.com

American Science & Surplus sciplus.com

Artbeads.com artbeads.com

Auntie's Beads auntiebeads.com

Beadalon beadalon.com

Bead Needs beadneedsllc.com

Bella Venetian Beads bellavenetianbeads.com

Chelsea's Beads chelseasbeads.com.

Creative Pals creativepals.com

The Earth Bazaar Merchants of Fine Beads theearthbazaar.com

Eclectica eclecticabeads.com

Fire Mountain Gems firemountaingems.com

Fusion Beads fusionbeads.com

The Gem Shop thegemshop.com

Grafix grafixarts.com

Hobby Lobby craftsetc.com

Jo-Ann Stores Inc. joann.com

JudiKins judikins.com

Knot Just Beads knotjustbeads.com

Kolo Photo Albums kolo.com

Legacy Scrapbooks legacy-scrapbooks.com

Little Windows little-windows.com

Michaels michaels.com

Midwest Beads midwestbeads.biz

Museum Tour Catalog museumtour.com

Oriental Trading Co. orientaltrading.com

Ornamentea ornamentea.com

Paper Source paper-source.com

Photofetti photofetti.com

Rio Grande riogrande.com

Soft Flex Co. softflexcompany.com

Crystallized Elements by Swarovski
store.swarovski-crystallized.com, create-your-style.com

Via Murano viamurano.com

Vintaj Natural Brass Co. vintaj.com

About Cathy

Originally from the Chicago area, Cathy moved to Milwaukee to attend Marquette University in the early '80s and never left the city. She began making jewelry more than 15 years ago, while working at a Milwaukee daily newspaper. In 2005, she landed her dream job as editor of *BeadStyle* magazine.

Cathy teaches beading classes at the annual Bead&Button Show in Milwaukee, and she frequently donates her beaded work to nonprofit organizations—primarily those that support the health and welfare of women and families. At *BeadStyle*, one of her initiatives has been "Beads of Change," how-to jewelry projects that incorporate products from third-world bead makers and nonprofit organizations, helping boost their visibility and sales.

In addition to making jewelry, Cathy enjoys travel, creating scrapbooks from her trips, baking, gardening, movies, and books. She lives in a beautiful, old house in Milwaukee that's filled with beads and memories—"and there's always room for more of both," she says.